HIGH WATER
EVERYWHERE

2nd Edition

GARY COPELAND LILLEY

Gary Copeland Lilley

05/08
22

Willow Books Classics

Willow Books, a Division of AQUARIUS PRESS

Detroit, Michigan

High Water Everywhere
2nd Edition

Cover photo: "Flooded_Greenville_Mississippi_1927." Public domain.
Cover design: Aquarius Press

ISBN 978-1-7379876-5-9

Credits: Poems from *The Hog Killing* were previously appeared in a chapbook by Blue Horse Press (2018).

Willow Books Classics

Willow Books, a Division of Aquarius Press
PO Box 23096
Detroit, MI 48223
www.WillowLit.net

Printed in the United States of America

Contents

THE HOG KILLING

The Preparatory Fire for the Hog

The air is sharp, colder than the shallow river that has started to freeze: a thin pane of ice growing just off the banks, the first week of January when the ground is hard, and the woods, a shame of naked trees shattered among the evergreens, deer beds in the tall brown grass on the other side of the pig pen fence, the enclosed grubbed field that doesn't have a root, blade of grass or a weed, and the family in heavy coats and mud-boots, an array of sharpened knives, an abundance of prayer, the early-morning work of harvesting pork—a twelve year-old boy hauls firewood to the steel trough where he will heat the water to scald the dead hog.

The Car is the Crucial Chariot

If you are twenty miles from a city and a dance every Friday night at Hillcrest Gardens, and you live a quarter-mile from Sandy Cross crossroad and the same distance in the other direction towards Joppa Baptist Church, and Bill Jordan's white liquor joint is five miles north of there but the Hillcrest run takes you instead down Low Ground Road, through thick piney-woods, and every now a pocket of houses to the south, to the bog where the big bucks walk the hunting season (the old folk say this is a haunted piece of land) on both sides of that short bridge barely big enough for two vehicles side by side, it's like a driveway that crosses over the blackwater river, and around the curve from there, in the cornfield stubble, in the gloam, the flock of wild turkeys gleaning the grain left by the combine, the nine graveyards on the low ground route, the separate boneyards for blacks and whites, at night a heavy fog always rises over this road.

The Choices for the Pistol and the Knife

The men have gathered around the thick steel rod at the end of the trough where the fire has been built and as usual someone has a pint of shine and it is passed around as they look over the hogs all gathered in the far corner of the pen—you can see the last breathes of every chosen animal; and every man, woman, and child has a job to do, the day promises to be as cold and hard as the ground they are standing on, and everything's alright because having enough food can keep you from feeling like you're poor, every man wiping his mouth knows that, knows how to deal with hunger that comes in a child belly, so two of the older boys are chosen, the one with the almost-mustache and the tall one home from the Army, they will kill the hogs.

The Moonshiner's Wife at Church

She can't take another beating, where the deacons? There ain't nobody here willing to step into the liquored sanctuary of his home and put a stop to this shit? She knows she can't keep letting her two boys see this. I can see the hurt in their faces, the deep furrows already in their brows, I can see them hating him. They young now but they already got that man musk and piss on their hands and I know it won't be long before one of them steps to him. And I'm sorry, I don't think she want either of her boys in prison for killing they father. A drinking man is bad business in a family. But a drinking man with an endless supply of whiskey is the devil's continuous flow of hell-stench into the house. He blacked her eye before church service, and then later got mad and beat her again because she went to the worship service without any make-up. Her boys, she got to save them, she don't want either of them ever treating their wives like that, she gonna have to make him quit, or kill him herself.

The Oh Marys Don't You Weep

The five married women are in the kitchen, skillet cooking slices of fresh pork which will be the sandwiches served for lunch with cold Coca-Colas; they laugh and joke about their husbands to the other wives, but nobody talks about any husband but their own, that is their code, no mentions of drunks, wife-beaters or ramblers, never ever any recollection of any other lover unless his name be Jesus, and the loudest woman is already working on the evening meal of more fresh pork, macaroni and cheese, string beans from the fall canning, pear preserves and scratch biscuits for desert, coffee with sugar and cream, the kitchen windows sweating from all the contained heat.

When the Boys Were Miss Pearl's Pallbearers

The six boys on Miss Pearl's porch were all wearing white short-sleeve shirts, without ties, because in late July it's too hot to wear black suits, and, except for the occasional fan of a hand towards a fly buzzing around one of their heads, they all stood as still as they could in the corner of the porch that was shaded by the huge pecan tree on the right-side of her freshly cut yard, no doubt it was done by one of the boy, they all had one or another regularly cut her grass, the mortician had earlier rolled Miss Pearl into her living room, his air-conditioned hearse was humming under the tree.

The boys, all of whom had regularly pinched their church offerings to buy the candy Miss Pearl sold between Sunday School and Sunday Service, knowing that she knows, and she forgives sins—her family was family these siblings and cousins sweating on the porch, and across the road a crowd of fifty people waiting in the near shade-less church yard, it seemed even the stunted chinaberry tree was trying to get under its own shadow, some of the men squatted under the brims of their fedoras, the women under umbrellas and parasols.

When the church bell tolled the boys went single-file into Miss Pearl's house, the white clapboards faded from generations of weather, slow-walked into her living room, her plastic-covered beige chair and sofa had been removed, her coffee table of Jet magazines placed under the window, the casket on rollers in the middle of the room, and when the boys came out they steadied their step, the air-conditioned hearse humming under the shade tree but they commenced to walking Miss Pearl across Joppa Road.

Snake-Handler

My son has been the Rattlers Assistant Defensive Coach about five years now, right after he played some college ball and used all that eligibility, never graduated, and there ain't no jobs round here and this don't pay that much but he got it, and he's a man who always got a Bible in the hip pocket, and trying to do right coaching linebackers—play hard, play fair, no cussing, and on the bus to the championship game the team was playing that music they listen to roll of thunder loud, cause they ain't had a history of winning seasons, we so small town we ain't even a town, we farmers, them boys were singing a song where he couldn't understand a word they singing, but they were together, and he could feel their blood pumping, could see the black warrior ghosting in their eyes, bigger and louder, and when they pulled into the stadium parking lot he told them: Get ready you dirt road boys, God-willing, tonight, we gonna kick the shit outta these city boys, and they cranked it up again my son said because the Lord will provide for the righteous. That's what I always taught him.

The Granddaughters and the Queen-Mother

The young women, and the girls, clean the guts delivered by the washtub-full, the blooded and blue-tinted ropes, the unfinished business of the pig steaming into the overcast day, a primal smell soon to be gone, bucket after bucket, washed in the cold water, and delivered translucent and clean to the matriarch who sits at a wooden work table set in the yard, where the boy has built a fire nearby, and she grinds the fresh pig meat, adds the salt, black pepper, a touch of nutmeg, the sage, sprinkles of parsley and red pepper flakes, packs it all and creates the links of sausage, the savory chains of before-sunrise breakfasts that will hang from the smokehouse rafters.

HIGH WATER EVERYWHERE

High Water Everywhere

Black water done rose around Sumner
Drove me down, down the line

Black water done rose around Sumner
And drove Poor Charley down the line

Lord, I'll tell the world the water
Done jumped through this town...

Charley Patton

The Sermon on the Piano

When there's this much devastation, and nothing much else but a bucket of blues in my heart, my default is to Professor Longhair, who this time points me to Dr. John. So, I put him on to atone for some of my sins (those other than the ones I've committed in New Orleans). That sanctified storm is just part the weather. His left hand complements the choir chords and lets the bass mark the bottom that I call home. Two truths always ride one song, secular and sacred is the crossroads. God stands in steel-toed boots, He's any tool that fits my hand. My good woman is gypsy jazz from the Spotted Cat, stirred in gin and sitting in the dark. She completes my keyboard, when we hold hands she restores my heart. The Crescent City won't die it's a honky-tonk, this ain't one long funeral march. Dr. John hammers and everybody swings 'cause every night has the spirit in New Orleans. So to all you swamp-dwellers most times lost, a piano brings both, good faith-good love. When you hear it then you'll have it, but you got to listen loyal like a dog.

Bishop Shelton and the Old Rugged Cross

I have to be honest with you, when I first came back and saw the devastation to my church, all that mud, all that foulness, I fell to my knees and wept. I am one of the chosen, my grief piled up like the gut from the houses. I've been a minister for forty years, but I lost my faith. I got angry, told God you want it fixed, you fix it.

How am I supposed to live? Am I not one of His apostles? My home in ruin and my sanctuary destroyed. Eighty years old and I am offered a job with the city, riding a truck and picking up trash. What had I done to be beaten so? Why had God, of my salvation and hope, allowed me to prosper just to snatch it all away?

I was on a crew of Haitians removing flood debris, and they never allowed me to get out of that truck to pick up anything. All day I rode the truck through the wards, seeing that swamp of furniture, swollen bibles, rusted pistols, color TVs, and then finally seeing the big picture; the righteous and the sinners, we all get hit with the same blessed hand.

Objects in the Mirror Are Closer Than They Appear, Part 1

I knew I was heading south, I just didn't know I was going back in time. But we pulled off the road at the Alabama Visitor Center just past the state line, and I sat in the shade of the magnolia trees with my shoes off drinking a bottle of cold water when I noticed the boy, Kareem, climbing the stainless steel pole, and then saw him remove the Confederate stars and bars that is the state's flag, a crowd of shocked white citizens gaping up at him, the afternoon sun beating down on everybody's head.

By the time I put on my shoes he was coming back to the bus. He said he couldn't stand anymore of that Dixie shit and had thrown the flag in the trash. I felt the long highway get a lot longer. By now, the white folks were looking at me like I'd done it. They called their children to the privileged shelter of their shadows as I approached. Some of the glaring men stepped into the paved path I was walking.

I pulled the flag from the can by the vending machines, folded it the best I could, and carried it inside to the info desk where a middle-age woman in a khaki uniform was getting the number of the Alabama State Police. I knew I couldn't let that stupid city boy spend one night in an Alabama jail. And if I let him go there alone I would never forgive myself.

My right hand was raised like I swearing to tell the truth in a Jim Crow court, I spoke to her, Hey, some of my students have been collecting souvenirs from every state we drive through, and they want to know how much would it cost them to buy this flag? The beads of sweat made a mustache over her open mouth. Everything froze, save the burning cross behind her blue eyes. That flag ain't for sale, she spit, and I laid it gently on the pale historic arm that was dialing the phone.

The Good News Gospel Quartet at Ray's Boom-Boom Room

Outside, with the Frenchman Street family—the blues people; the mix-blood musicians from the bayou and the city, and the two gin drinking, ballad singing women who run the show in their high-heel boots and fedora hats—the gospel singers are comfortably chain smoking with the group of angels in front of the barroom window. The laughter fits the evening as easy as short sleeves.

A five dollar cover charge and every table is full. Inside spilling music, Charlene, the barmaid, who plays basketball for the University of New Orleans and spends enough daytime in the weight room to righteously stretch that muscle-shirt, and who customarily slays men and women every night every time she throws back the dreadlocks and shows her delicate face, she comps the spirituals their four double shots of tequila.

Cell-phones vibrate, it's 11 o'clock, and the evening is just getting started. Ray is serving plates of barbeque and jambalaya, and is giving up the take to help put the lighting back in their gutted church. A few of the random Indians are playing the set and *Fire on the Bayou* runs through the house. Big Chief Doucette gives a shout out to the gospel boys who will soon be gracing the mikes harmonizing it won't be the water next time.

Shelter in the Time of Storm

I want a wife who can pass a drug test. Everything is disposable, the flood showed me that. All relief workers in Saint Bernard come to my bar cause Camp Hope just down the road. Yes indeed sure as I'm telling you. It's put me in debt up to my neck but I own four apartments and this bar that was under the water. Those house-gutters come early evening, college kids on break, most of them still wearing their steel-toe boots, slipping dollars in the jukebox and dancing with their drinks. Now, I am a devout Catholic, and a coon-ass, too. I'll sell a beer to anybody who come down here to help us. Hell, them college kids gets one free. Look at these day drinkers, poor bastards. They out of work off the fishing boats, and not a one trying to leave the only place they think they belong. Ain't enough crab and shellfish left to even feed that black cat that found her way to this place. Ain't nothing and nobody in good shape no. Right now every damn soul in here fears God, it's like the happy hour was all the day long.

Whole parish was under the water, and if you can show me anywhere else in the blessed U. S. of A. where the entire county had flood I'll give you a case of whatever you drink. Folk down here don't leave all they own just 'cause of hurricane. So the wife and I didn't. We stayed in the apartment on second floor where I'm still living right now. We could fix food but we didn't have no light no. Every building and shed still standing on dirt smells like the canal, like death and petroleum. Other than refineries crack dealers were the first people to rebuild their business around here. There barely a dry place for them to stand but they make sure you can find them. And then the thieves came. That's when I lost the wife, just too much strain. Her church all boarded up with that goddamn red X painted on it. Even the cemetery was closed. Tomb doors opened up in all that water and them bodies just floated away. Now, you tell me that right there ain't truly dead and gone.

Drink a Little Poison (Before You Die)

It wasn't about aim. It was about the pressure, the blue note, the bending of the 3rd and 7th notes, when Saint John's grandfather played his black Silvertone on his front porch, singing *Drink a Little Poison* sitting in a straight-back chair, a pint of Sloe Gin by his tapping right shoe, an open invitation from the approaching twilight, the deadline when all of last night's juke joint promises can still rightfully be reconsidered.

Saint John's grandfather said he aimed to please and would play any tune we wanted to hear. The sun slipped across the canal and lit the downtown silhouette, and under the streetlight, that unsettling cloud of bugs, all the mistakes I'd collected in my spell of time on earth. I reached for the gin, Saint John beat me to it, tossed the cap into the street, tipped it up and drank a hook, and then passed that dying soldier to me.

That night I believed in blues and gin, and my casual aim was to just have fun. But somewhere between the warm booze and the delta slide of that Silvertone, chances had it that I could come down sick for offering a woman more than I was going to give, and if she happened to be friends with a hoodoo mean enough I'd be drinking muddy water, sitting on a hollow log, I'd be the dirty dog every mother except mine thinks I am.

1202 Low Ground Road

Everything gone, birth certificates, the high school diplomas, my grandmother's portrait, the family Bible, everything that was a record of who we were, gone to fire. The kitchen where my mother wrote obituaries for all the families down our road, military veterans and long time deacons, mid-wives, drunk drivers and drive-bys, Eastern Stars, and the missionaries who'd sat nights of final moments with so many others, the clock radio she locked on gospel, the straw broom in the corner, the cordless phone, the oak table and everything above it gone to char. My mother begins to weep. The vanity and all the hand mirrors, her closet of hats and coats, the red shoes she wore to church and club, the mahogany dresser with the framed picture of the three brothers in suits leaning lazy against a car, one stabbed in Norfolk, Virginia, another shot for going there and asking the right people the right questions, murdered weeks apart. The revolver's grip and the night stand, the hope chest, the four poster bed and her quilt, all now gone to flame. The crowded parlor, books reduced to ash, the white porcelain figures, praying hands, swans, and bells scattered on the burned floor, the blue reclining chair and sofa, the color TV, the love seat with a ghost of smoke sitting in the front yard.

Swannanoa

I'm in the last booth my usual spot, my back to the wall so I can face the front windows and look out on the parking lot. All the day shift people know me, they know I'm the All Star breakfast, a cup of coffee, cream no sugar. I'm the slow walk to that jukebox where every song cost a quarter. Three plainclothes cops are at the counter asking Betty what she knows about the escaped con that stopped by and had breakfast, and she said he fit right in with all the meth heads, Vietnam vets, and college kids. He got the steak and eggs, hashbrowns, begged a cigarette, paid for the meal with cash and left a 5 dollar tip. She said nobody, not even Johnny Law was going to make her give that back. All three of the cops try to stare her down. She winks walking away, telling them that their black coffees, as usual, are on the house but their donuts will be one dollar each.

Saxophone on Yvonne Dupree's Backyard Fence

Didn't I drink a hurricane in a French Quarter bar that never had more than a half-foot of water out front? And did not I wade through the tourists buying novelty charms in the voodoo shops as I searched for High John? Did I not watch the Indians march through the dancing exile crowd and the motorcycles parked all down Jackson Street? I cleaned up a vacant lot and gave the police the rusted gun frames and the mud-covered ammo box that was under the only remaining doorstep. Have I not seen Survivor's Village outside the projects where they won't let the folk return? Every soul in a tent needs a private Moses. And didn't I see the black mold spreading likes a community rash as people prayed for their living rooms as the politicians sipped the FEMA water and prayed for casinos and condos. I saw the Mississippi River, and I pulled the innards of an old gray house towards the curb after placing the family crystal, the salvaged wedding silver, the china dinner plates, a coffee can full of wet money and insurance documents on a white tablecloth laid before the tarnished saxophone caught in Miss Yvonne's backyard fence.

Objects in the Mirror Are Closer Than They Appear, Part 2

After 2am, when the bars close, it gets busy. There is one black waitress in the diner. She is efficient with the late night crowd, refills their coffee cups like she's reading minds. The rest of the staff don't pass small talk with her, the other waitresses cut their mascara eyes. The cook doesn't even look at her when she gives him the orders. On the grill he slaps the bacon, cracks eggs into the skillet, and wipes sweat with the tail of his apron. Most of the men in the smoking section that is her station look her up and down, and give dirty answers when she asks if they need anything. One of the white college kids is a regular and you can tell from the hope in his face that he would like to get to know her. He offers polite conversation but she doesn't give anybody there that kind of attention. When the action slows she takes a cigarette break, goes alone out the back door. The college boy finishes his coffee, lays a three dollar tip on the table for her and leaves. The older waitress, a set of weather-beaten luggage sagging in her face, walks to table and wipes the crumpled money into her thank-you pocket. She knows everyone sees her, and she knows none of them are going to say anything.

Hoodoo You Love

Juneteenth, and the only thing they're selling in the park is beer, whiskey, and water. In the canopied shade of the VIP section black politicians, ministers, and celebrities are eating catered food. We are regulated to the mass outside the ropes by a chicken wing eating guard. My woman is a minority here, and I feel her tighten like a wire fence on account of the crowd being dark and deep, and the lingering smell from the muck of last night's argument.

But we are relief workers in the Crescent City and this celebration marks the day the slaves in Texas learned that they were free months after the Civil War ended. No one told them you see, and today we are juking it up and it is still just a small hallelujah to whatever the newly freed might have done. Brass bands from around the city have gathered and the possessed are moving like they're being hit with switches. An intoxicated man gets in his mother's face and starts cursing her. There is way too much liquor flowing and the sun is way too hot. The sisters are giving my woman grief because what is Miss Jane doing with a black man in Louis Armstrong Park. The boldest one is dancing in front of me in tight jeans and a halter top, doing the African moves I've seen in Harlem, DC, and on the Discovery Channel. Dear God, Lil' Miss Kim I am old enough to be your poor papa.

But the music makes me dance, my feet start moving. My woman sees that, gets a bit twisted, and it is then that I deduce that I have made a mistake. I have danced with her griefers. So, I ask my woman if she is hungry. I know the road home, I've seen the signs, atone, I know it leads here. She uncrosses her arms, nods yeah, and I step off with four-years worth of faith that I will find a place nearby that sells pulled barbeque with mustard-based sauce, squares of bread pudding, ice cold Coke Colas, and hand-rolled cigars.

Holding Counsel on Mau-Mau from the 7th Ward on the Fourth of July

He still barbeque. Look at all this meat he bought. He was cooking pig in the middle of the night, spreading out those hickory coals, pork grease burning off in the pit. You can still smell the smoke. Say his mom ain't never do drugs. She ain't unfit. But she got men who show up every now and then like they got the answer for everything. She ride on the shit they say like it's a limousine. Look at them, mouths full of food, holding beers like they had something to do with this. Say he love his mom but she got to have more sense when it comes to men. She tell him they said if he take a bust right now he get sentenced adult so he better get out of the dope game. *That's* the big news from her felony friends? Fuck them. Think he don't know that shit. They need to be talking to *their* kids. He got two little brothers and a baby sister who ain't doing nothing but spending what mom makes, he's the one bringing home the cash. Say he dreams of good money on a regular job, you pay him enough he'll serve you fries at Mickey Ds, but he ain't sweating himself wearing polyester for chump change. Say he got to man-up, you understand? He got household bills to pay. This one-way street, this his spot, and he can't let no police run him off.

'Round Midnight

She is radiant, utterly in the roux, and that's when I'm feeling amazed, like I'd been pouring myself into a glass over a sugar cube, and then the answered prayer, the combustion, the wonderment that the one person in this room I am in love with is still bending an elbow with me. This is the Garden District blues, the hour when people will start showing their tattoos, and all the fresh scrubbed out-of-state hurricane following contractors will think that there's still plenty of time for their near-nasty talk when the music cranks down to the ballads and slow songs, and that's when she invites me out into the New Orleans humidity to smoke a hand-rolled cigarette. I slap my Zippo down and across my jeans, come back up with the flame, and put fire to that stick of possibilities. Absinthe will splash along the dark bar 'til morning and we don't give a damn in this swamp of moonlight, we are the fallen, from North Carolina, snaking the apple and on our way back inside, in love in front of the bayou band, and we dance the two-step real close, just like we'd done all of this before.

Wade in the Water

I drive the ugliest car in my entire family: including my cousins, and elders. I have an old Ford van with a wrinkle in the front left fender and compression dents along both sides. The salt rust from the hawk winter has migrated with me from Chicago to Carolina and blisters up beneath the fading brown paint. I drove my van from the Blue Ridge down to New Orleans, my fourth trip after Katrina. I'm staying at a minister's house on a corner that had been under seven feet of flood and on my way there I stop at a po' boys joint and buy a pack of cigarettes. Even though I can't afford to have any habits sometimes you've got to do things just because they give you pleasure. New Orleans can make you feel like that. In a neighborhood that is now mostly waste the desire for immediate relief can be the want for a bottle of water.

Near the canal the grass, vines, and yellow weed-flowers move like a savannah in the lower ninth yards empty of all but steps and foundation stones. Decay is in the air you breathe. I haul the wheelbarrows and tools and help gut a house on Independence. Shoes, mattresses, furniture, toys, and soggy clothes are the base of the mound at the curb. The black mold. The warped hardwood floors, chunks of the sledge-hammered plaster, bags of pulled pink insulation and broken slats of lattice get dumped on the pile and the home reduces to a frame, the water-rot of everything hard or soft. When the gutting is done I drive my van to Frenchman's Street because I prefer drinking bourbon with the local stubborn who love the city. I stay awhile and slake the dusty day.

At the small park between The Spotted Cat and Ray's Boom-Boom Room, two musicians, an old trombone player in a black suit and tie, a stingy-brim hat, and a teenager in baggy clothes, and wearing shades even though it's near midnight, plays the trumpet, and they lay down the roux for the vocalist, a long thin dreadlocked woman in black denim. Her eyes are closed, and what comes from her is the river, and the 'bone and trumpet are soon caught up in it, and the certainty of the blessing washes over everyone. The band are all clearly from the same family, they have the same dark skin, the same thin face, and this devotional river song can only come from them, beautiful them. A battered five gallon bucket sets on the sidewalk in front of the band like an open dream book of numbers, and every tuned-up soul that wades by drops in a few bills.

Lil' Willie and the Playground Blues

Some big boys when we go to school they take our money. They never nice to us. We always nice to everybody but round here we just little people running through busted bottles, crack bags, and way tall grass in the park. Every time I find a bike and fix it up somebody steal it. My best friend use to live across the street now I don't know where he is. We shoot ball like crazy even in those bent rims. Got to pick up crawdad trash, and that stinks, just to play a game. Ain't no swings on the swing. Nobody come to take care of this place. They say there were bodies floating here when it was flooded. We didn't see that cause my brothers and me were at the Superdome but at my Grandpa's funeral I saw Auntie slip a silver dollar for the other side into his coat. We live in a FEMA trailer in our old front yard, and after school we stay outside 'cause it so small. When we playing we have beaucoup fun till the big boys come. Sometimes they come in late and don't care that we already here. Acting like we ain't ever going to grow. They like termites from a rotten house that's been pushed down, a buzzing cloud round the streetlights. They sell drugs. They fight. They cuss and bust they empty forties on the court. They always try to go somewhere dangerous with they blunts and they guns and that's when we lil' folk got to get on home.

Death Takes No Vacations in This Land

The spring equinox is on Good Friday this year, and the dogwoods are in bloom. I see the white flowers in the forest wherever the morning sun reaches the ground. Folklore from the elders of the Negro church says the cross for the crucifixion was made from this tree and since then it hasn't grown straight enough to cut another beam. I choose to believe it even though I know that the flowering dogwood is not native to Jerusalem. My father, who to me grew shorter every year, a wife-beater and chain smoker, is 77 and in the hospital with three blocked arteries to a heart I didn't know he had. My car has a blown gasket, water is leaking into the combustion chamber and it stumbles down the road. I don't push it. I check the water and the oil, and drive it easy around town, rethinking the email from my sister with the phone number for his hospital room. I do not want to call this man. I don't want to give him another shot at the hole in my head, the chance to parade my ex-wives into a conversation about the price of gas, not one more occasion to glean the field of my deficiencies and place the bowl of spotted fruit on the table before me. I don't want to give him the last nasty word. I want to send a branch of dogwood, a gnarly twisted limb with the white flowers that mark the end of winter, a blooming cross to bear, a seasonal sign of the after-life, the promise of victory over our fast approaching deaths.

Objects in the Mirror Are Closer Than They Appear, Part 3

The Odd Squad, that's what the rest of the crew used to call me and Frankie. Whenever the ship pulled into a port, and we would go on liberty, I was sure to be wearing a dashiki, and it was a known fact that he'd be wearing his Dixie flag ball cap. That's just the way it is. He's from West Virginia, and who in America knows if I'm from Angola, and then the Bronx. Ain't no aircraft carrier truly integrated. You keep to yours. So, always, just inside our earshot, everybody, the whites and the blacks, ask the same dumb ass question, *What the hell is a soul brother doing hanging with a redneck?* Simple, he's my friend, and my ancestors were forced to mine for diamonds and gold, and his people were forced to mine for coal. Frankie didn't mind being called a redneck one bit 'cause the name comes from miners on strike tying red bandanas around their necks to identify the righteous from the scabs. But still, he would cold look them in the eye while pulling hard on his unfiltered cigarette, and then drawl out something provocative, like, "Don't be so douchie 'bout physically expressing yo'selves, if it truly bothers yall that much." The ship's crew knew that we're down with each other if anyone decides to make the move. Every bar we stepped into, on both sides there's always an empty barstool. Before the night was done we both usually drunk and standing back to back, fighting every sailor, civilian, colonizer, and scab who refused to respect us people who come from under the ground.

I'm the Best Dressed Beggar in Town

I belly to bar like I'm the last of the regulars. There's nothing but asses on the barstools. I take the middle and all heads turn towards me, the only person here from The Great Dismal Swamp, and I am much cooler than their brand new refrigerators.

I am the stranger who comes in honor to the crows. Wearing my black suit, you can measure me to be an undertaker, or otherwise size me up as dangerous. I order double-bourbon neat with a glass of water on the side. I return all the hard looks and soft eyes coming my way.

I'm the Marlboro in a room full of organic cigarettes. I got no dust on my shoes and I've been leaving all my change for the barmaid's tip. Blacks and whites are dancing to the Revealers Reggae Band. This is the one-love crowd, we all have big smiles.

A woman takes the space in the middle of the floor. On her finger is maybe the slimmest of wedding rings, but she is by herself, dancing like she is due for better circumstances, and the room spins with heat and humidity when she looks at me, like I am somebody she wants to know.

Hank Medford, Bulldog Security, Drinking Free Coffee While Commenting Out Loud About Bobby Johnson

No white man should have to work like him: a goddamn fry-cook, a sneer of black tattoos up each arm to the bony shoulders. You ought to see what my daddy and granddaddy worked for. They got paid like niggers. That's the kind of stuff probably pushed this excuse for a white man into cooking meth at a trailer park lab. Stacking that paper as people's teeth was falling out. That shock of hair spilling underneath his dirty ballcap looking like an order of home fries scattered. Six months from the joint and his parole officer already is sticking tight to his dumb ass because she, like me, don't believe that he's settling for minimum. Gold- chaining it up high end white-trash style he was. Mr. Bobby Bucks. Heard it got him ten years, how time flies, but I see he's still got that goddamn gold tooth. Bet he didn't smile so much with it those days. Right now I say he still makes more than he made in the penitentiary and that was more than he deserved. I see a white boy like him I righteously just get pissed. Says he wants to keep hisself out the central lock-up. Everybody knows that this time of night is big business, and drug trouble had best be too busy to come eat fried eggs in this diner. And it's my job on this late-shift to make damn sure of that.

As Far As You Can Go Without a Passport

New Orleans, 1996, on that visit I stayed in a bed and breakfast that had grapefruit trees around the backyard breakfast patio. Dreadlocked and unshaven I ate like I was used to having fresh fruit picked and served with my eggs. I was a twenty-hour drive from the America I knew: taxation without representation under Papa Bush, Cheney, the Gingrich contract, the Dick Armey, and mandatory sentences for third-strike crack. Cruz had given me the off-season rate and was serving me in his customary white linen suit. He was the personal newscast I'd been listening to every morning for three days. So, I knew that Congo Square is now Louis Armstrong Park and that the drums are not played much there anymore. And I learned that the Voodoo shops did not completely cater to non-believers, therefore, I could still buy the High John root. I lit one of the cigars I'd bought the day before from a cigar store near Jackson Square after watching the exiled Cubans hand-roll them. And while enjoying my coffee and chicory every morning I learned that inmates from the city jail hose and sweep the French Quarter streets before the tourists come out. Cruz told me it was surprising how good they all look when they're incarcerated and wearing those baggy red jumpsuits. But I was from DC, and I know there's nothing pretty about doing time. The five black boys cleaning the street were singing so low I could barely hear their hip-hop blues, and the career corrections officer driving the truck looked hung over, so he kept their pace slow and easy.

When the Saints Go Marching In

My whole life has been one long fight, the day to day, hand to mouth. All the opportunities to roll over and die, each promising moment, can carry the dead weight of generations. So, I know why folks in New Orleans love their football team, a who dat month of mistakes between wins mojo band and their original paper-sack-over-the-head fans. New Orleans earned the name, "the city of the Aints."

After the flood, their run of God-touched victories, the redeeming Saints remain and the team is kicking all the big asses. The people in the wards who chose to stay, and the families blown across the country, are all wearing their black and gold. Not even Mr. President Bush can kill New Orleans, they tough enough. The testament of their hoodoo history and their pirate's heart are always on display.

But the road to The Superbowl is long and as difficult as the road home. This team has to face the Bears. And I have lived in Chicago, where there is no glitz and glamour, only hard work in the slaughter-house winter, where a city refused to be consumed by fire or corruption and police, where the blues first went electric. Season after season of almost, in the sweetness seats at Soldier Field, on Sunday in Chicago everybody prays.

But here in New Orleans, at Lucky's Bar and Laundromat, where I drink and wash clothes, the Pre-Game is on and they are serving hurricanes, two for the price of one. I am a guest relief volunteer and, with respect, I have left my Bears cap on my sleeping bag. All the Saints are in black and gold, flipping-off FEMA to free bowls of gumbo, and everybody in New Orleans knows that the struggle is the only promise to the faithful.

Good Morning Heartache

I wake to heartbreak; it's my family car following the body to the funeral. There's no need to wait for the alarm, it's crack of dawn early, and the school-boys are not out yet cupping their cigarettes at the bus stops, only the lazy are still lying in their beds.

This year began as smooth as a Buick and now I'm smoking her forgotten cigarettes, smoking the old letters stamped with a drop of her perfume, the sepia-shaded emptiness inside my party clothes. No food, no booze, no dope, or poem satisfies since she left.

The furniture factory that is in my head starts work while it's dark: hung-over drivers drink cafeteria coffee and hair of the dog, raw oak is pushed into the band-saws, a night club veneer sprayed on every slat, the heavy freight of loss is rolled and stacked and waiting on my loading dock.

I think of her every time I drink water. I see myself in her mirror; the long tooth missing, the white stubble of beard before I shave, and the gray at the temples that show my age. I may be the hardest face that ever graced this downhill street, but good morning, heartache, I am walking.

THE BLUE HIGHWAYS

The Blue Highways

Iraton is my old man and his younger brother
could not say his name through a stutter
so he called him I.T. for the short pronunciation
which I had teenage-shortened to "It" who drove truck
in the logwoods and on the independent long haul
after moonshine put the roadmap in his hands
and on one cold Saturday when he was home
from the whiskey run through DC, Philly, and New York
I walked down to the garage that serviced
his rig where Monk who I played football
against every season when our two rival teams
met on the rocky fields of one or the other
segregated schools we attended fixes the flats
to earn extra money for the juke joints
we had never tried to avoid was waiting for me
so we could plan on picking up the girls
and going to the beach to see Bobby Blue Bland
sing Cry to Me like he had just made that song
to mark our glorious arrival in Monk's '62 Ford
Starliner and that red diesel cab of the truck
was in one of the bays with the hood up and no one
in attendance and shouts were coming from behind
the garage where "It" was in a sweat stomping at a man
who had crawled halfway under a junk car
trying to avoid those scuffed and grease covered
heavy trucker boots that had probably seen
about 100,000 miles of highways and bad roads
and when I ran up Monk was standing there
looking ashen which is difficult because he is dark
just like me and that's one reason we became friends
because everyone was always calling us blue-blacks
and acting like we should be ashamed of that
and we wont and grew our big afros

to give the term capital letters but Monk
starts trembling with a half empty bottle
of Nehi Grape soda dangling in his hand and says
that's your daddy kicking my daddy's ass
and he turns and throws that bottle at the junker
cracking the sun-spotted windshield and "It"
swings around cocking his fists to see who else
wants some and spots the boy beside me who
backs away and never speaks to me again.

On Breaking Up

Every sailor who sets foot on the ship
has already accepted the act of his drowning,
but no one on a fishing boat knows when the submarine
is beneath him, and there lurks as much a possibility
of its fairwater planes snagging the steel-cabled nets,
pulling the boat backwards in the rough seas,
swamping him, as much as there is that the morning
will find the catch secured, and him heading to shore
smoking in the wheel-house, the certainty of coffee
already on the stove, but now, as he heads out
in the cloud-covered night with nothing but the knock
in his motor fading over the ocean, he is going
to have to plot the course with the scars every sailor has,
towards an horizon of fractures, fires, radio failures
and hydraulic malfunctions which will all seem pale
when compared to the pressure of water.

The Spell to Get Rid of Snakes

The Forestry Service released hundreds of king snakes
to counter the state's eastern region rodent problem.
Big snakes were at the landfill, and in the barns.
Snakes under every structure near the edge of woods
and in the tall weeds up the slopes of ditches.
Every fifty yards saw a snake flattened into the asphalt
like a road marker on the route to hell. As far as my mother
was concerned, she'd rather have a pantry of mice than a snake
anywhere near her house. She had divorced my father twice.
He only took that final decree serious after she pulled
the pistol I had given her when I was in the navy
and came home with that gun and she had me show her
how to use it. She had simply refused to return it.
He said nothing. Beneath his receding hairline, from the corner
of his eye he could see the cartridges in the cylinder
of the pretty combat revolver she had taken to toting
in case she found any snakes anywhere she walked.
My father said that nothing could never be sharper
in a critical moment than the smell and gleam of gun oil.

The Matriarch: Our Lady of Low-Ground Road

My sister's cancer, I am the one who called mother
with the bad news, then told her how hard it was
for the others to break it because two of her sisters
had passed this way, and not one of us wanted
to give her this parental burden, but my mother,
who graduated from nursing school after she retired
from quality control at a fragrance corporation
and every year had given us the perfumes and colognes
we still use on the days that are special to her,
like Thanksgivings when we are all expected to gather
in appreciation of our simple blessings on being alive,
my mother got on the phone with John Hopkins, the best
hospital she knew to get the skinny on their chemo
and radiation treatment before she conference-called
all her children in a prayer for my sister, beginning God
steps in after we have done all that we can do...

Gettysburg

The October woods were red and gold
past the fence lines of rolling pastures
until I got closer to the battlefield of shops
selling more souvenirs of the rebels than
New York Yankees ball-caps, then I was there,
at the most haunted farms in America,
the fallen of both sides are now the landlords
of this soil. On Seminary Ridge, the long crooked
stretch where the Army of Northern Virginia
camped with their cannon aimed toward the blue
of Cemetery Hill, I slept that night out in the open,
until the rains came. A cold slow hiss on the fire,
the shrouds, the dark clouds gathered in, I moved
my bag under the modern shelter, the picnic area.
A steady rumble of rain over the grounds and I couldn't
sleep, so I sat on the bench by the dead fireplace
from four in the morning 'til the touch of dawn.
I expected some gray ghost to saunter up
and respectfully join me as I marched
through the last cigarettes in my pocket because
the currency that has been paid for me, a black man,
to be there shivering in the Pennsylvania morning
is more monumental than the stone that honors
the North Carolina regiment that fought
and died opposing my emancipation, more stately
than the statue of Robert E. Lee and his horse.
Three death-filled days acknowledged by all
mark the resurrection of the free Jesus
from the tomb, John Brown standing on the gallows
of white man's laws. Like it or not, pray with me
or not, or share the can of beer floating

like a spirit in my cooler, everything
I have done or will do in America
has been paid for with blood.

The Lamentation of Saint John Brown

This is a hard road, Lord, you have me ride. My children have died while I was not at home. Now it is my time. The coming day will be a test of my faith, and it will find me heaven bound in the army of the righteous. I am in bondage to my oath to remove the great sin from this land. I shall wear my sorrow like a brace of pistols. I cannot completely trust a man, black or white, afraid to die in the commission of God's will, fearing to drink from the bitter cup and break the chains. That weakened heart, that disappointment has long been a quality of the abolition forces. They put out a pamphlet and talk in the halls and churches, where even the Friends often judge a Negro to be criminal for the violence of liberating himself from under the oppressive hand, and they deliver him, for this offence, to the slavers to avoid prosecution from the law. There is no higher law than God, there is no sterner judge. I bloodied my hands in Missouri, Lord, fighting slavery I have cut the unjust to pieces. And now, Douglass, who purchased his freedom with coin, rides from the camp before the morning breaks at Harper's Ferry, having failed in his mission to recruit slave troops from the plantations. He rides out with less than grace, Lord, through slave territory, dreadful and alone in this hell, but he does not look back.

The Blue Ridge

I left Provincetown with an overloaded
ashtray, in a rain of thirty days, the wind
blowing it horizontal off the Cape.
My old Ford van needed a quart
of forty weight oil to keep it from knocking
like it was the law. There's no beer or bourbon,
just coffee and Red Bull for the ride. Heading south
the radio stations static out every fifty miles
and I'm the old friend exiting the party.

In DC I drive past saxophone ghosts, spiked
punks and post-riot bluesmen grinning
outside The State of the Union, boarded up
with a For Sale sign stapled to the plywood.
I swing past the F. B. I. building, the corner
where Flora Morton played her national steel
gospel, believing God could still hear it from there.
Her family, thinking her crazy, was surprised
after her death when the congregation of street
artists and agents paid for her tombstone.
I take the by-pass around Richmond turning gray
in the afternoon, and there is no doubt
that I am positively in Dixie, the loblolly pines
casting long shadows across the road.
I've been gone from Black Mountain six weeks
and there's still six more hours pushing these
expired tags. I turn off my cellphone
because I know that my good woman
is aggravated, and I am driving above
the legal limit to whatever waits for me.

Tamaqua Heritage Day

It's a 19th century passenger train that departed
from under the shadow of John Kehoe's hilltop grave,
at the depot with the old broadsheet newspapers
shouting murder and Molly Maguire, and click-
clacked through the Tamaqua tunnel, a blasted hole
in the rock, and then sunlight dapples again across
the seat I'm sitting in.   A tourist from Kansas
has found the Abe Lincoln impersonator,
and introduced him to me, the only black on board,
and then the quick flash of the digital picture
is his emancipation.   The school-kids riding
the festive rails are mocking the steam whistle
like a chorus of wolf-pups whenever the train
rounds a bend. An old couple— her blond hair
now mostly white, and him wearing a comb-over
that starts around the right ear and rises
towards the west like a crown—they lean into
each other and he kisses all the sunspots on her face
before he moves to her lips, and the school kids
who see them hoot and howl as the train moves
through a crossing where a young man stands
over his bicycle and waves like a metronome,
and one of the school-girls waves back.

Summit Hill Cemetery

On the ridgeline: yellow autumn trees
move in the wind like a field of grain
waiting for the tractor, the anthracite
is buried beneath the slow dramas
of everyone who can hear the drone
of a small plane in the striated clouds
over the boneyard stretching to the Lehigh River,
neighborhoods, the dead communities
of the Slavic Orthodox, the Protestants
and Catholics, flag-flying Americans
all with their feet towards the rising sun
in the land of the continual dangerous dance,
the breaker boys and miners, the bosses
and barons, and the true religion found
either in the pocket or in the pits and
dark shafts where they harvest the coal.

Black on Black

I can see this truth even in the drizzle rain:
under the streetlights blue glow of halogen
fresh blood is blacker than night.
The police move slow within the yellow tape.
I don't know the boy lying here knocked loose
from one of his high price basketball shoes,
his bony forearm a confusion of tattoos,
the gold tooth that still flashes like a beacon.
His brown eyes unbalanced, the left bulges
more than the other. The head shot from the right.
His slack body does not respond to his mother's call,
and that woman wails. There is no other way
to describe this. She stands between two friends
on the cracked sidewalk and they hold her up.
They all have that stressed urban environment look
that comes with raising hustler sons, their big eyes
light the entire scene, their faces are contorted in disbelief.
And they let the woman wail. She screams wide
as her mouth allows. The police chalk circle
brass casings that dot the street, and give them numbers.
The gathering crowd, you can smell the foul
excitement of blood. It is a contagion, gunshot wounds
mutate and multiply, this year, 300 homicides.
Folks in the crowd acknowledge friends
and relations in the flashing blue and red light
that reflects off the slick pavement, one black cop
is busy taking photos of everything and everyone.

Deer Hunting

You don't shoot a deer swimming across the river,
they'll just drop under the water and all the game
is lost. So you wait and shoot when they reach
the opposite bank. I didn't know that the first time
I went hunting. I was thirteen and in the cypress swamp
posted up behind a stand of brush, my back to the river,
the sixteen gauge shotgun a cold piece of steel in the damp
and fog loaded and laying heavily in my arms, the barrel up
and expectant like I had just been taught. My father
had forded the river downstream at the bend where
it was slow and shallow and was now on the other side.
We are in the woods two weeks before the season
poaching for food. While dark he had walked
into the boys bedroom with a cup of black coffee
and said this is yours if you want to get up right now
and help me feed the family. In the moonlight
we left the house in silence and were soon flying
down the blacktop, the gray grizzle on his face
riding over the sags. We had parked the pick-up
on the wide shoulder of road just past the bridge,
clicked the doors shut without slamming them
and walked a quarter-mile into the bog. It was strange
to see him in the crow morning without a Marlboro
in his mouth but I didn't know then that he never
smoked in the woods. When we could hear the rush
of the black river we separated, him moving softly,
a ghost in the mist with a twelve gauge pump
in his hands. He was calm as I had never seen him.

CAPE FEAR

Introduction to Cape Fear

While travelling in spring of 2006, I read a tiny notice in a prominent national newspaper, apologizing for its participation, as part of the propaganda wing, in a campaign that led to the 1898 massacre of African Americans in Wilmington, NC. I had never heard of it. It was not taught or talked about in the state. I was born in North Carolina, and returned to the state when I was twelve to live in a segregated community and to attend its segregated schools. I did not understand why we blacks were living under a system of apartheid. I am grateful to the Commission on the Wilmington Race Riot of 1898 for the research that uncovered this buried history. The self-proclaimed White Supremacy Campaign ended Reconstruction, and put muscle into Jim Crow. The Wilmington Race Riot of 1898 laid bare the social conflicts that arose with constitutional change: the hopes of newly freed black citizens juxtaposed against the desires of southern whites to preserve the antebellum ways. Its leaders became the state's governors and congressmen. The Wilmington Race Riot of 1898 altered the trajectory of freedom, and remains the only coup d'etat in American history. I thank the Commission for their diligence and enormous courage, inspiring me, and giving me fuel, a moral obligation for a native-son to tell this North Carolina history as poetic dispatches.

Gary Copeland Lilley

Colonel Waddell on the Morning of November 10, 1898

They vote Republican black. They walk
Our streets with their heads up, with more freedom
Than a white man, and now we have been made
To conduct our city's business under
The rule of carpet-baggers and negroes.
White men will suffer eternally
If we do not honor that it's our blood
That makes North Carolina sacred ground.
If we don't act they'll soon have the land
And all our grand history that's on it:
The Confederate graves, all the gray men
From all our families, to their proud deaths
Give glory, honor the white way of life.

Let black bodies choke the Cape Fear River.

The Shade of Prosperity

Hope is a hammer in the hand that builds
the foundation of the house that can withstand
the storm. It is the expectation of tomorrows.
In 1890, Wilmington, North Carolina's largest city,
was home to seventeen thousand negroes
and eight thousand whites. It had streetcars
and electric lights while most of the state
was still stuck in darkness. Negroes owned
the most successful and competitive cotton compress,
and ten of the eleven restaurants were owned by coloreds
who had always cooked the meals that plantation
whites ate, but they had been the servants and now
it was a business. The negroes owned twenty
of the city's twenty-two barbershops. Coloreds
were the jewelers and watchmakers, tailors
and mechanics, wheelwrights, blacksmiths
and masons, plumbers and plasterers.
Bell and Pickens, a negro company, shipped
one-fourth of all the oysters and fish
to markets along the eastern seaboard.
Thomas Miller, a negro, was one of the city's three
real estate agents, and Frederick Sadgmar
was a wealthy contractor and architect.
The *Record* was the nation's only daily
negro newspaper. Its editor, A. L. Manly,
the mixed-race son of a former governor,
encouraged all colored men to exercise
their constitutional right to vote.

On the Cape Fear River

Inland from the sun rising off the Atlantic coast,
past the cypress of the Southern Dismal Swamp,
you come upon the city, once the last supply line
of Robert E. Lee's Confederate army. Railroad
and shipyards; the industrial hub for mill towns,
lumber camps, cotton plantations, and tobacco markets
across the state's coastal plains. Whites with small farms,
with the same sharecrop concerns of the coloreds
who walked behind the mule and plow, the populists,
had joined the Fusion coalition and the Democrats
thereby lost control of the state, and now negroes
even held public offices in buildings they had previously
not had a presence. In Wilmington, coloreds and whites
contemptuously shared the same sidewalks, went to
the same shops, in the neutral spots of blight they lived
in the same neighborhoods, and most whites considered
these reversals of their lives to be domination:
three negroes on the ten-member board of aldermen,
a colored justice of the peace, deputy clerk of the court,
superintendent of streets, a colored coroner, a number
of negro policemen and mail clerks, there was an all-negro
health board and two negro fire departments,
President McKinley appointed the negro John Dancy
as collector of customs. Wilmington, where the white men
who could speak, who could write, and who could ride
gathered following the election of 1896 and moved
to restore their natural order; this is where
North Carolina's White Supremacy Crusade begins.

Mrs. Rebecca Latimer Felton's Call

Where are the white men? In the past
few weeks have they not heard as I have,
the stories that colored men attack and ravish
white women on the farms, and the only impediment
to this foul act, it seems, have been the few occasions
the negroes were put to the tree. Where are the brave
southern white men when there is not enough
religion in the pulpit to organize a crusade
against sin, nor justice in the court house
to promptly punish crime, nor manhood
enough in the nation to put a sheltering arm
around virtue and innocence? If it takes lynching
to protect a woman's dearest possession
from the ravening beasts—then I say lynch,
if necessary, a thousand times a week.

Alexander Manly's Editorial Reply in *The Daily Record*

Poor white men are careless in the matter
of protecting their women. Especially
on the farms. They are careless of their conduct
towards them. Our experience among poor
white people in the country teaches us that women
of that race are not more particular in the matter
of clandestine meetings with colored men
than the white men with colored women. Meetings
of this kind go on for some time until
the woman's infatuation, or the man's boldness,
bring attention to them and the man is lynched for rape.
Every Negro lynched is called 'a big burly black brute.'
In fact, many of those who have been thus dealt with
had white men for their fathers, and were not only
not 'black' and 'burly,' but were sufficiently attractive
for white girls of culture and refinement to fall
in love with them, as is very well known to all.

August 18, 1898: The Democrat Response to the Editorial

It was immediate. Manly's words, considered insolent,
vile, and defamatory, were exactly the fuel needed.
Never have white men stood by passively when anyone
would seem to suggest that their women sometimes seek
sexual congress with colored men. And for a negro
to say this is to imply his conquests, which could never
be anything but an assault upon those fair and virtuous
Southern women unfortunate enough to cross his path,
his words were nothing but boasts about his brutish ability
to rape their wives and daughters. The allusion
of such a crime dooms a negro to the rope, to the fire,
and in this white men across the state stood strong,
shoulder to shoulder in a defensive ring around
the flowers of the south. The white men of Wilmington
came together to protect the sanctity of their homes.
Colonel Roger Moore, who had distinguished himself
during the Civil War had been placed in charge
of security by the Secret 9, and the entire city
had been zoned and sectioned, and each colored segment
was patrolled nightly by the Red Shirts for the better part
of a year. The words of the negro Alex Manley galvanized
white men to the white supremacy cause, and gave
the Red Shirts an insufferable offense and the whiskey
of revenge riding towards the election.

The Fire, November 10, 1898

The Red Shirts, two thousand devils twelve abreast,
marched into the colored neighborhood,
to the corner of Seventh Street, to the Love
and Charity Hall where the newspaper was printed.
Alex Manly was already gone having been warned
that his life was in danger. They set upon the building
and lit it up. Flames went through the roof and sparked
nearby houses. The colored fire crew
responded to the call and tried to fight the fire
until the armed white men cursed and shot
above their heads. They would not let them near
the *Daily Record* and the office burned down.
A grandmother dropped to her knees
in front of the African Methodist church
and called on her God to destroy these white men.
Some flames cannot be doused, the colored children broke
from the school screaming and ran through the streets.

The Waterfront

The harvest from the longleaf pine, the pitch
and turpentine, and the lumber yard,
the railroad offices and the shipping firms
were all located at the mouth of the river.
Sprunt's Cotton Compress on Front Street
employed hundreds of coloreds—laborers,
machine operators, and stevedores
to load bales of cotton onto the ships.
It was a regular morning until they heard
the fire bell ring, and some of the wives
ran into the building to tell their husbands
that the *Record* was burning and white men
were shooting, and setting fire to the homes.
The workers left their posts and were standing
in the street sorting through their confusion
when a stevedore said that the white folks
should not stir them up, that they had no
right reason to terrorize them as they were
all just church-going working men.

The Killing of Carter Peamon

Mr. Hugh MacRae, of the Secret 25, the Ku Klux Klan,
and a decorated veteran officer of the Confederacy,
having been informed that a mass of rowdy negroes
were at the Sprunt Compress, sent a delegation
to determine if it was true that they were arming
themselves. He sent Mr. Heiskel Gouvenier,
a copperhead who had settled in Wilmington,
and a squad of sober Red Shirts with repeating rifles,
and the 70 year old negro Carter Peamon
was pressed into service to lead them there.
The negroes at Ninth and Nixon Streets
took the white men hostage, and intended to give
some return for the terror that they had witnessed.
Carter Peamon came to the defense of the white men,
and after several hours arguing for their lives
obtained their freedom and escorted them back
to the safety of Mr. MacRae. When they learned
of the threat the white men received the drunken
Red Shirts wanted to hang the negro until Mr. MacRae
insisted that would be wrong, but they should banish
him from their fair city. So the negro Carter Peamon
was taken to the depot and was on his way to exile when,
it was said, he jumped from the moving train, and
subsequently was shot dead by an unknown white man.

Fourth and Harnett Streets

The colored workers from the waterfront gathered
at George Heyer's store, smoke from the burning
of the *Record* heavy in their clothes. A streetcar load
of Red Shirts came to the Brooklyn neighborhood,
and they disembarked to confront the coloreds.
Curses and threats flew from the opposing corners
of Fourth and Harnett Streets. Mr. Aaron Lockamy,
a newly sworn white policeman, under orders to arrest
no white man, tried twice to get the coloreds to leave.
But they would not. He told the whites that none
of the colored carried guns. But they didn't care.
Officer Lockamy left the scene wearing the cloak
of his official inability. One shot, and then a volley
was directed towards the coloreds. Sam Gregory
and John Gregory were killed right there. Sam McFarland,
who was on his way home to dinner when gut shot,
crawled underneath Mrs. Strauss' house on Fourth Street,
and died some hours later. Two of the wounded stumbled
into a home on Harnett and the white men followed.
Inside they found a dead man, and another unidentified
negro with grievous wounds. The rest of the coloreds,
those that could, escaped west down Harnett Street.

The Gauntlet

Daniel Wright, a negro politician and leader,
an example of colored dignity was implicated
in the wounding of Mr. William Mayo, who was
shot through both lungs in the cross-fire directed
on the coloreds running down Harnett Street,
even though there was no reliable testimony
that the negro Daniel Wright had been there.
The Red Shirt mob demanding surrender shot
into his freshly painted house. It was then
that the negro returned fire, killing Mr. Will Terry and
Mr. George Bland before the Red Shirts captured him.
The negro was hit in the head with a length of pipe
and made to run the gauntlet. Before he ran
fifteen steps he was riddled with bullets
and laid there in the street for most of two hours
before the Red Shirts allowed some of the coloreds
from the church to remove him to the hospital,
where he was denied treatment
and lingered for a day before he died.

The Machine Gun Squad

The gun, paid for by local businesses, was secured
to a wagon donated by Orrell's Livery Stable
and pulled by Mr. Peter Harris' flop-ear mule.
It was a rapid firing Colt which could discharge
over four hundred .23 caliber bullets per minute
and was manned by a squad of out-of-uniform boys
from the Wilmington Light Infantry who hadn't seen
one bit of action during the Spanish American War.
It was their white supremacy platform well oiled
and hauled across the Fourth Street Bridge
into the Brooklyn section where the poor whites
lived mixed into the colored edge. At Sixth
and Brunswick the boys said they believed someone
shot at them and they returned fire, killing
twenty-five negroes at that intersection, and under
the leadership of Captain William Kenan
they proceeded to Manhattan Park where they fired
into a house, killing the three negroes inside.

The Cool Deliberation of the White Supremacy Campaign

Not one white man wearing a red shirt
was without a score to settle with a colored:
for having a job or a position in city government,
for being the instrument of the vicarious insult
of getting arrested by a colored policeman,
for knowing how to read, for not lowering
their gaze when approaching white women,
for acting like equals, for not stepping off
the sidewalk in their presence. A marksman
of the Wilmington Light Infantry set fire
to a Brooklyn shack and shot nine coloreds
one at a time trying to escape the flames.
A deaf negro boy was shot dead for failing to obey
a Red Shirt command. At the Cape Fear
Lumber Company six colored workers were shot
and their bodies buried in a nearby ditch.

Before the Night is Done

Word came that the colored men from Navassa,
the small village west of the city, had rallied
and were coming to aid the coloreds in Wilmington,
taking a route that would have them crossing
the Hilton Park Bridge. The machine gun squad
rushed there to cut them off. The coloreds did not show,
so if they came into town they'd chosen another road.
At dark, small groups of negroes had gun battles
with the Red Shirt patrols that rode through Brooklyn,
firing volleys with shotguns, hunting rifles, and pistols
and leaving before the machine gun could get there.
The resistance of the coloreds was as big a surprise
as their successful tactics. Then the Red Shirts, armed
with Winchesters, walked the neighborhood
block by block, shooting at every negro caught outside
and searching every negro found at home.
The possibility of their own deaths a rising moon
riding every red shoulder. There was a report
from two undercover negro Pinkertons
that the coloreds were at a negro church
distributing weapons and organizing their defense.
The colored leaders were identified as Josh Halsey,
Tom Miller, and Josh Green, and it was clear
that one of them said, "Before this night is done
I will wash my hands in the blood of a white man."

The Exodus

As the *Record* burned the colored women
fled their homes, children in tow
to the outskirts of town. There the few men
who'd escaped the patrollers joined them
and made their way towards the marsh.
They rested in the cemeteries, with their backs against
tombstones or lying stretched along the graves.
The mild November day grew chilly, and at dusk
the cold mist from the river rolled in. The roads
were filled with the refugees carrying their bedding
and a few personal belongings, and the children
whimpered as they quick-marched with their mothers
into the darkness of the night, into the bog.
Crouching waist-deep in the icy waters
a pregnant woman gave birth to her baby
who then died from exposure. It began to rain
and the negroes continued deeper into the swamp.

We Have Taken the City

The Red Shirts led a cross-section of white men
to the City Hall—the pastors, the merchants,
and the stumble-bums who usually spent the day
drinking near the wharf—and they demanded
the resignation of all the white Republican politicians.
Mayor Silas Wright at first refused, until the din
from the crowd became too loud, too murderous,
to ignore. Likewise, one by one, the Republican aldermen
then resigned. Colonel Waddell agreed to serve as Mayor.
The Police Chief was fired. The colored police officers
were stripped of their guns, badges, uniforms,
and dismissed. Mr. George L. Morton, commanding a troop
of Red Shirts, rounded up six prominent negro leaders
and under bayonet point, and the threat of death,
marched them to the northbound train, bound
for exile. The Republican whites considered to be race-
traitors were arrested and then ordered to the train.
One of whom, Mr. G. Z. French, was dragged
to a telephone pole and a noose on Front Street
when he was given a reprieve, and allowed to crawl
to the train where he crouched beneath the seat
as it pulled away from the station. From the white
churches, where all the white Christian men had taken
the solidarity oath and swore to see the campaign
through to the end, the bells tolled throughout
Wilmington, and Colonel Waddell announced
to the white crowd, "We have taken the city."

Acknowledgments

The poems of "The Hog Killing" appeared in earlier versions in the chapbook of the same title which was published by Blue Horse Press.

The poems "The Killing of Carter Peamon," "The Gauntlet" and "Before the Night is Done" were published in *Home is Where: An Anthology of African American Poets from the Carolinas*, editor Kwame Dawes.

The poems of "Cape Fear" previously appeared in a chapbook of the same title which was published by Q Press.

Grateful acknowledgements are given to the following journals in which these poems first appeared:

The Cortland Review: "The Lamentation of Saint John Brown"

Minotaur: "Gettysburg"

Willow Springs: "Colonel Waddell on the Morning of November 10, 1898," "The Fire," "Fourth and Harnett Streets," "The Exodus"

Black Renaissance: "Objects in the Mirror are Closer Than They Appear, Part 1," "Objects in the Mirror are Closer than They Appear, Part 2," "Objects in the Mirror are Closer Than They Appear, Part 3"

Ecotone: "Saxophone on Yvonne's Dupree's Backyard Fence," "Bishop Shelton and the Old Rugged Cross"

Red Line Blues: "Wade in the Water"

Peal: "1202 Low Ground Road"

About the Poet

Gary Copeland Lilley is the author of eight books of poetry, including *The Bushman's Medicine Show* (Lost Horse Press, 2017), a chapbook, *The Hog Killing* (Blue Horse Press, 2018) and the first edition of *High Water Everywhere* (Willow Books, 2013). He is originally from North Carolina and now lives in the Pacific Northwest. Copeland Lilley has received the DC Commission on the Arts Fellowship for Poetry and is published in numerous anthologies and journals, including *The Best American Poetry 2014, Willow Springs, The Swamp, Waxwing, Taos Journal of Poetry and Art* and *African American Review*. He is a Cave Canem Fellow.

CPSIA information can be obtained
at www.ICGtesting.com
Printed in the USA
BVHW05032815042
634375BV00001B/48